Reflecting Pool

Susan Spaeth Cherry

CHICAGO SPECTRUM PRESS
LOUISVILLE, KENTUCKY 40207

For Fane from the Philippines
and Angelique from Rwanda,
who have enlarged my reflecting pool

CONTENTS

THE OTHER SIDE
OF UNREQUITED LOVE

It never leads to desperate measures,
like groveling or jumping out windows,

never inspires symphonies
with oboe solos and dissonant codas.

No one writes ballads or sonnets about it.
Its roles on the stage are cameos.

But being unable to love the one
who worships all you do and say

is like dining on a luxury cruise
where you gorge on lobster, *boeuf en croute*,

chocolate mousse and flaming meringues
till your body screams *too rich, too much.*

You picture the whip of emptiness
walloping bellies around the world

and guilt begins to bubble
in your stomach like the pink champagne

the waiter serves you day and night.
You learn to say *no thank you*

with a graciousness that makes you choke
and scan the horizon for land, any land.

DAD AND DAUGHTER PLAY DUETS

Side by side, they sit with eyes
affixed to swarms of dots with stems
that speed across the page like cars
continuously changing lanes.

Their clarinets embrace and part,
embrace and part again with ease,
the very essence of the love
they've shared for her eleven years.

He stops to switch her *C* to *A*,
to pencil-beat a rhythmic hitch.
She asks him to adjust her reed,
teases him for a mistake

while I, her mother and his wife,
listen in the room next door,
knowing I will never hear
music more magnificent.

Black granite panels piled with names
mirror the faces
of curious tourists, many too young
to remember Kent State
and *Hell no, we won't go.*

Beneath a can at the base of the wall,
a note: *Hey, buddy, here's that Coke*
you never had the chance to drink.
A youth scans lines of chiseled letters
dense as the type in a James Joyce tome.
He finally finds his father's name,
pencils a rubbing on colored paper.
A middle-aged woman, certain now
that the man she loved will not return,
drapes a cross with the MIA bracelet
she's worn since 1968.

Cell phones unborn in the time of My Lai
battle like soldiers from opposite sides.
Pot-bellied veterans cluster on Harleys,
blowing smoke rings into the dusk
as their radio blares today's casualties
in Baghdad, Fallujah, Kirkuk, and Tikrit.

SUNFLOWER

You peek
into windows
for tidbits
of gossip
and scoff
at begonias,
impatiens,
and pansies,
who cannot see
a speeding
police car
or fire truck.
You boast
that Vincent
Van Gogh
was your lover,
flaunt your gold
like a Hollywood
mogul, look
down your nose
at the daisy,
your plebian
cousin.
But soon
the trees
will rob you
of your fourteen-
karat finery.
Your haughty head
will hang
with shame,

and from your eyes
a thousand tears
will tumble out
for birds to eat.

CHAIN

In a windowless basement
designed to hide
my tumble of toys from upstairs eyes

I scissor paper into strips,
trying to stay on the rulered lines
I've struggled to space an inch apart.

I twist off the top on my jar of paste,
caked at the rim like the nose of a child
with a runaway cold,

cover the tip of the wand with white,
and dab it on a strip the hue
of the pumpkins my parents

will carve at their party
when I'm in bed tomorrow night.
I press the ends to form a ring,

grab a strip of shiny black,
and loop it through the first as if
the two of them were holding hands.

Another strip, and then another,
orange and black, orange and black,
intertwined like life and death,

until my chain is long enough
to wrap around the do's and don'ts
that shackle every eight-year-old.

STAYING AT WORK
ON A SNOWY EVENING

(with apologies to Robert Frost)

Whose firm this is we lackeys know.
The partners make a lot of dough.
The richest is a racketeer,
A connoisseur of *quid pro quo.*

The game is on; I want a beer,
But to advance in my career
I have to work without a break
Like every future financier.

I fear my wife won't be awake
When I get home. She doesn't take
My hours well. They make her weep.
But there are deadlines I must make.

The window calls; I'd like to leap,
but I have email thick as sheep
and piles to go before I sleep,
and piles to go before I sleep.

RESCUE

The dining room table is dressed to kill,
with yellow roses in its hair. The boy
in a miniature suit and tie
fidgets in his Queen Anne chair,
running his hands through unruly curls
asleep beneath a Brylcreem quilt.
The ant-women scramble from stove to trivet,
casseroles in their mittened hands.

He puts his napkin in his lap,
making sure his mother sees,
and bows his head while grace is said.
Every plate is in its place. The silver
gleams like a smile from God.

Reaching for a serving spoon,
he accidentally taps his milk,
which topples like a gentleman
stricken with a heart attack.
Panic hastily invades, armed
with reprimand and shame.
Sponges, rags, and papers towels
charge out of the kitchen like cavalry.

As he stares at his shoes through a salty haze,
his grandfather flicks an arthritic thumb
at a nearby crystal water glass.
Icy liquid meanders across the tablecloth.

Grandpa turns to him and winks.

SELF-CONFIDENCE

Crater-laden,
it waxes and wanes
as it casts back light
another supplies,

wobbling
as it circles existence,
its Ocean of Storms
and Sea of Tranquility
thick with the salt
of experience,

changing
from the hottest hot
to coldest cold
and back again.

E-DATING

We know so little
about each other,
know only that possibility
swims between
our computer screens,
its scales shiny,
its gills open wide.

I type and delete,
type and delete,
a cub reporter terrified
of asking something
out of line.

I run the spell-check,
click on *send,*
then check my in-box
every hour, hopeful
as a Sunday hymn.

In a week or two
we may realize
we have nothing in common
but keyboards and mice.
But for now, let us savor
the taste of maybe.

THAT SONG!

It steals into your frontal lobes,
perhaps while you are showering

or paying your electric bill,
and starts to chase its tail.

You throw it random tidbits
from the pantry of your day,

desperate to distract it,
but it circles like a Hula Hoop,

pausing every now and then
to lick its leg or scratch an itch

while your gray matter changes
to neon pink. Then suddenly

it falls asleep, bewitched
by the goddess of sanity.

OUT OF IT

Evening stitches
the day's last scraps
into a quilt of quiet
as we stroll the streets
we've sauntered down
a hundred times
while dinner dishes
cried for soap
and coffee dripped
like liquid night.

You flare and dim,
flare and dim
like fireflies
that cross our path,
asking *Where are we?*
again and again
as though you were
a tourist here.

I point to landmarks
you should know—
the grocery store,
our children's school,
the house where once
you helped a neighbor
build and urethane a deck.
Of course, you say,
and shake your head
as if attempting to unroot

the tumor growing
in your brain.

I chatter to distract you
from the agony of lacking
and lead you toward
the glow of home
while blue turns gradually
to black.

TURNING FIFTY

5 and 0
side by side
like the husband and wife
in *American Gothic*

somber
as they hold the fork
of the unknown

Heel-to-toe
I teeter across
the top of five, terrified

of falling off and landing
with the hook
around my sagging neck

or even worse

of getting wedged within the 0,
unable to move
like a car in mud

Five plus zero
equals five

Five minus zero
equals five

Five o'clock shadow
Five stages of grief

Five senses
Five pointed star

Fifty

NOT ENOUGH

She kicked in my womb as if she knew
that life outside was hard as the face
of a prison guard. But out she came,
red and robust, to be flannel-wrapped,
lullabied, and nursed on an overflow of love.

When classmates at her nursery school
excluded her from playing tag,
I smoothed a Band-Aid on her heart,
assured her there'd be other games,
but knew my words were just umbrellas
rendered useless by a gust.

When her father, in the prime of life,
left her for Persephone, I baked
her favorite pies and cakes,
loosened the nooses around her sleep,
held her hand as she trudged through the slush
of daily musts— knowing my deeds
were not enough

and will never be as the future stumbles
down her street like the village drunk,
sometimes babbling, sometimes flinging
empty flasks.

THIRTEENTH SUMMER

Her name was Isabelle,
chic these days
but not in the era
of Ladybird Johnson,
Peyton Place
and Man of La Mancha.

The Lindas, Barbaras,
Susies and Debbies
called her
Isabellybutton

and mocked her glasses,
her greasy bangs,
and most of all
the saddle shoes
she wore to camp
with bell-bottom pants
ringed in ruffles
of neon pink.

I heard her scream
the day she found
the toad they'd hidden
in her bunk,
saw her teardrops
when they tossed
her parents' letters
in the lake.

Stop!
I yearned to yell
but I,
who couldn't swim
or float alone,
was silent
lest they throw me
from the deck
of their acceptance.

To Isabelle I dedicate
this poem as an apology
for all the things
I didn't say
that summer many years ago

when being liked
was a full canteen
and doing right,
an empty one.

FINANCIAL WORKSHOP

Around a chipped Formica table,
cornrows gobble powdered donuts,
veils devour apple Danish,
dotted foreheads gulp sweet tea.

Blue eyes peer at nostril pierces,
shoes with soles that gape like zeros,
sweatshirts stained with baby spit-up.

Brown eyes fix on pearl earrings,
patent pumps with matching purses,
leather portfolios stuffed with handouts
telling how to weave success
on deprivation's wobbly loom.

Women all, synonyms
with lungs and hearts and ovaries
yet unalike as breasts and brains,
every one with much to learn,
every one with much to teach.

THE CAPTURE OF SADDAM

Last evening, hailstones and sleet
blitzed the spring with mastery.
We closed our curtains, built a fire,
sheathed our feet in fleecy socks,
ignoring queasy thoughts about
the fate of open crocuses
and buds in buntings tightly zipped.

Today, we woke to tinseled trees,
to Nature bathing in champagne.
We poured it in our coffee cups,
drank and drank without restraint

until our eyes were much too glazed
to see the branches on the grass,
the flattened shoots, the green turned gray.

PHARMACOPOEIA

Beneath a roof of yellow plastic
shingled with the seven days,
tablet tribes and capsule clans
assemble in adjoining rooms.

Muscled uncles pin the limbs
of chronic pain, cousins
pummel seizures with persistent fists,
aunts wield brooms
to shoo away despondency.

You howl about the way they bounce
your innards like a basketball,
rail at them for roping you
forever to the hands of clocks.

But I embrace this mix of kin,
sure that if it takes its leave,
the life we share will cease to be.

SESTINA FOR MARIA

She calls it *our land* but never *home*,
that sea-cupped country boiling in fraud
like an overcooked dumpling, a place
where her seven children wait
for her to cook them a better life
from scratch in a kitchen far away.

She cannot will the fears away
of robbers stealing from her home,
of ransoms on her daughter's life.
She smiles, feeling like a fraud
but knowing those on whom she must wait
think complaining is not her place.

She takes three buses to the place
where visa pleas are thrown away
by those who've never had to wait
to tuck their children in at home,
who think the foreigner's a fraud
intent on swindling American life

of its riches. But restoring life
is her only aim. Each week she'll place
bouquets at the altar, praying that fraud,
like her modest blooms, will wither away,
that Jesus in his heavenly home
will deign to shorten the torturous wait

for her children's papers— and after the wait,
which feels like death, will come after-life

as warm as the sun in her island home.
She has trouble recalling the look of the place,
a photo whose color is fading away.
She frets and frets that the game of fraud

will tantalize her sons, that fraud
will tell her daughters not to wait
for mother (who has gone away)
to parcel out the prizes of life.
She keeps spinning the dial, but is stuck in one place
on a board where the winner must land on *home*,

spins for her children at home in fraud,
who place their faith in her and wait
while the spring of their life meanders away.

PAINTED

On the plaza between the tattooed arms
of the art museum, I sear in the sun
of late July like a beach umbrella,

one of a dozen mannequins
spaced far apart so each can star
on his own little stage.

This morning, as always,
I combed the *help wanteds*,
then showered for hours in silver paint

until I became a man of steel.
I set my empty money box
within easy reach of the camera-clad

and took my designated place, forbidden
to scratch or go to the bathroom
or silence my stomach's demand for a sandwich.

Here I will stand till the man in the moon
tucks the tourists into their beds,
moving only the folds of my brain

as I conjure up my college days,
when I scoffed at Hermione's trying to pass
for a statue in a Shakespeare play.

ON BEING A CHILD

And as I was green and carefree...
In the sun that is young once only,
Time let me play and be
Golden in the mercy of his means.

–Dylan Thomas, Fern Hill, 1946

Dylan ripened on the tree of privilege,
listening to Shakespeare sonnets his father
read aloud from tomes as thick as the fog of Wales,
eating bowls of sugared bread his mother had made soft
in milk. His wishes raced through the house-high hay,
or so he wrote. But sons of luck no longer
can be princes of the apple towns, can only

gobble burgers
in the SUV while riding
from the soccer field
to the skating rink
to the piano teacher's studio
before they are deposited
at kitchen tables
piled house-high
with worksheets due
tomorrow at eight.

Dylan heard the tunes from the chimneys,
the music of calves who sang to his horn,
and was happy though his bedroom lacked
a single trophy or framed award
or medals hung like eyelids long deprived
of sleep. His dingle was ablaze with stars,
perhaps because he never
was expected to be one of them.

THE UPS MAN

Year after year he paces the streets
in his doorless truck, sporadically stopping
to drop a box on someone's stoop.

He never strolls like the mailman,
always runs as if terrified
of being consumed by suburbia's maw.

Sometimes he waves as he passes by
in his cocoa-colored shorts and shirt.
I smile back, but we never speak

until today, when he rings my bell
and hands me a package he'd usually leave
behind a pot of geraniums.

*My son was asked to play the sax
in a famous band,* he declares as his face
illuminates like a Christmas display.

Congratulations! I exclaim,
but before I can garner the details,
he races to his vehicle,

leaps into the fraying seat,
and disappears like a wonderful dream
that ends too soon.

DÉJÀ VU

Swaddled in my own fatigue
I used to rock my newborn son,
beseeching slumber to still his squalls.

But when the infant finally slept
I couldn't rest for fear that death
might sidle in and steal his breath.

I'd sneak into the nursery
and watch his chest ascend and fall,
exit and return again,
obsessive as a song refrain.

Tonight I hold my restless spouse,
transformed from father into babe
by cancer cells that wail beneath
the flimsy blanket of his skin

and once again I beckon sleep,
which comes for him, but not for me.

THE PASSIVE-AGGRESSIVE

dresses in tuxes,
in spotless shirts
with extravagant ties,
in shoes reflecting
others' faces.

He sets your table
with open roses,
explains the specials
with smiles that blaze
like kitchen fires.

The passive-aggressive
serves you steak
grilled longer
than you specified
but not enough
to be sent back.

He splashes you
with Beaujolais,
then wipes the stains
with napkins dipped
in goblets of apology.

When the passive-aggressive
brings your check,
you can't tell if
he's padded it
or if your math
is incorrect.

Feeling just a little
sick, you leave
the customary tip.

IN BALLROOM B

King Arthur must have planned this banquet,
for here I sit in a room of tables
round as the "o" in Camelot,
shouting my name across a kingdom
of water glasses and baskets of bread.

A cavalry of appellations
charges across the starched white cloth
but halts before it reaches me.
I turn to the diners closest by,
a monosyllabic man in tweed
and a woman intent on stuffing me
with details of her latest vacation.

Stuck as a drawbridge whose drunken keeper
has fallen asleep while winding the chains,
I smile and nod as obligation
overtakes my castle of patience.

WHY I STAY

Yesterday was hot and damp
as my collie's mouth. Today,
in a sweater, I stare out the window
at pink and white magnolia petals
marathoning on the wind. The sky
is the shade of robin eggs
but the radio, like my sinuses,
forecasts rain for the next five days.

I hear the chant of southern climes
that never scowl, that always smile:
Chuck that slicker, those waterproof boots,
those mittens you have worn for months,
and thoughts of moving shower my life,
puddling my serenity.

But weather that never removes its jewels
cannot replace relationships
I've formed here over forty years—
relationships solid as Midwest oaks
yet flexible enough to wear
a T-shirt today, a parka tomorrow.

I phone my next door neighbor
and invite her for a cup of tea.
Her voice is warm as the Florida sun.

THE MUSIC OF TERROR

Amid a pack of picnickers,
I nibble berries, bread, and Brie

as winds, percussion, brass, and strings
plant the park with flowers of sound.

Suddenly a helicopter
loops the lawn like a rondo theme

and a choir of sirens I cannot see
collides with the orchestra's harmonies.

Drums begin to beat in my chest;
gongs and cymbals batter my brain.

Once, before the Red Alerts,
the rolls of duct tape and plastic sheeting,

the basement rations of bottled water,
tuna fish and toilet paper,

Mahler's First would have muzzled the mouths
of every nearby ambulance,

would have silenced the growl of propellers
as it lifted me into a golden sky.

But now I hear only the music of terror,
devoid of rests and double bars.

THIRTIETH HIGH SCHOOL REUNION

After foraging stores for the perfect dress,
the perfect shoes, the perfect purse,
I spend a day at the beauty salon,
leaving painted, exfoliated,
a changed-for-the-better lady who once
wore granny glasses she didn't need,
tie-dyed bandanas, and loops of love beads.

Hesitant, I enter a ballroom
bedecked in our alma mater's hues.
China and silver shine on tablecloths
stiff as the drinks at the open bar.
Chandeliers reflect the gleam
of straightened, laser-whitened teeth.

The phrase *You haven't changed a bit*
flits from lip to glossy lip,
a butterfly alighting on flowers
whose petals are dropping one by one.

Leaning on a metal cane,
a hunchbacked woman dodders in.
The room goes mute as if on cue.
She approaches me with a crooked smile,
and suddenly I recognize
my favorite friend from grammar school,
transformed from elf to worn-out shoe.

Extending my hand, I notice a wisp
of auburn hair upon her neck

and realize her blue-gray curls
are just a wig. I scrutinize
her liver spots and droopy lids,
the work of makeup's magic wand.

The two of us begin to laugh
as a fellow alumna saunters up,
scans my friend with scandalous eyes,
and exclaims, *You haven't changed a bit.*

TAKING CHARGE

Frantic with the need
to flee
the hearth where cancer
scorches every
word and deed,
the child dons
a pair of boots,
sheathes herself
in wool and fleece,
and sizzles
into brittle night,
where ice benumbs
the angst of leafless
shrubs and trees
and darkness
masks a skyface
that has long forgotten
how to smile.

The wind coughs blood
that stains her cheeks
and cakes itself
upon her nose;
the snowdrifts loom
like frozen ghosts,
inhibiting her every move.

Plunking backwards
in a bank,
she sneers at Him
the world extols—
then pendulums her limbs
in white
to make an angel of her own.

A REFUGEE RETURNS

Armed only with courage,
he quits the camp
where children pick through piles of shit
to salvage undigested bits
of corn to boil into porridge,
where flies alight on still-warm corpses
already robbed of their battered sandals,
where rumors race through the spaces between
tubercular coughs and childbirth screams.

He steals past the border guards,
inhaling danger instead of the by-gone
scents from pots of cooking cassava,
not caring that the land he planted
has yielded mines instead of beans,
eager just to roll in the dust
he once called home.

MY DAUGHTER PLAYS
THE PLANETS

The stage is a score
of buzz cuts and ponytails
clustered like chords.
Gowned and bejeweled,
my daughter tunes,
binds her eyes to the baton
as if her survival were tied to its moves,
and depicts her sixteen years in sound:

Mars, the Bringer of War

She bursts from the womb
with the turbulence
of a lovers' dispute.

Venus, the Bringer of Peace

Sucking her thumb,
she sleeps in her cradle,
tranquil as a lily pad.

Mercury, the Winged Messenger

She flits like a bee,
anxious to sample
untasted nectars.

Jupiter, the Bringer of Jollity

Her laugh is a cache
of emeralds
as she rolls down a hill.

Saturn, the Bringer of Old Age

She boards the bus
to sleep-away camp. My gut
laments, "She's growing up."

Uranus, the Magician

Her gangly body,
straight as a freeway,
changes into a cloverleaf.

Neptune, the Mystic

Tea leaves brew
in cups that must cool
before she sips.

LEAVING FOR HOSPICE

With stagnant ponds
you stare at the strangers
who strap you to a padded chair
and hoist you down a flight of stairs
in a house where memories peel off
like paint exposed too long to rain.

They grumble that they need a smoke,
complain about their baseball team,
ignore you when you ask and ask
Will I see this place again?

The youngest pillows your head and neck,
tosses a blanket over your legs,
and orders me to open the door.
I ask if I can ride with you.
He tells me it's against the rules.

I grab my keys and follow the flash
that flies you to your new abode.

ESCAPE TO IRAQ

Miles below the DC-10,
the town of his boyhood tosses and turns
beneath a dirty sheet of cloud,
too tired to work, too troubled to sleep.

He gazes into lapis blue,
finally free of factories
that gasp like patients
plagued with fatal maladies.

Reclining his seat, he envisions himself
cool and suave in his new fatigues
and dreams of the thrill of the battlefield,
where no one is ever buried alive

in rusted steel.

WATCHING THE ARTIST AT WORK

She sweeps the canvas
with strokes as free
as a fantasy.
I speak to her
but she doesn't hear
my nouns and verbs, trifles
in her world of shapes
and planes and hues.

She squeezes white
from a wrinkled tube
and mixes in
a dab of black.
Steady fingers
ringed with gems
of inventiveness
make wispy lines
with bristles thin
as feline whiskers.

I scrutinize
an expanse of red,
a circle of purple,
a patch of gray,
trying in vain
to understand
a language
I have never learned,

then seat myself
at an easel of keys
to paint a universe
with words.

RITUAL

The plates nap in the kitchen sink,
neglected children
dressed in dinner's discarded rags.

I fill the kettle, retrieve the mugs,
yours the one with a Siamese cat,
mine, with a Pekinese.

We rummage through a basket crammed
with motley teas—
green for you, black for me.

The flimsy bags
expand and float like lily pads,
fragrant in a swirl of steam.

We sip our brew as if the clock
had lost its hands
and giggle at your dream last night,

chat about your math exam,
nibble bits of gossip
rich as slivers from a block of fudge

until our cups are empty
as my heart will be when Fall decrees
that you, my youngest, have to leave.

A TRUE STORY
for Jerri Cobb

She knew at twelve
when she flew in the back
of her father's plane
she was really a child
of Helios.

She hung around airports,
feeding and washing
birds of steel,
dreaming of being
the first of her sex
to blast into diamond-
studded black.

When she finally applied
for a mission in space,
she soared on every
test they gave.
But it was a time
when women were planets
orbiting men,
when stars didn't twinkle
for stars like her.
They sent three males
to the moon.

Yet when she heard
the *Eagle* had landed,
she eased her airborne
Aero Commander

laden with medicine,
seeds, and clothes
for those below
who'd never fly

into a tangle
of Amazon jungle
and danced a jig
across its wings.

STARTING OUT

Twenty-two and finally freed
from the permafrost of earning A's,
my daughter dons the optimism
I've given her in ribboned boxes.

She's lovely in her dresses of dreams,
her pumps of trust, her scarves of belief.

I snap her picture with my heart,
frame it in my yearning
for a world that will furnish
all the blessings she deserves

and hang it in my living room,
over a widening crack in the wall.

ENERGY BALANCING 101

Into the classroom the women flow,
a current of Gucci, Dior, and Versace,
oscillating with sundry symptoms
their shrinks and physicians cannot cure.

The teacher asks them each to choose
a colored vial to match her mood.
He croons, *Permit the subtle shades*
to vibrate into your sacred spaces.

He doles out bobbins that hang from strings
of dental floss like pocket watches.
To find your blocks, suspend your pendants
in front of your centers of energy.

The students dangle the cylinders
before their faces and hearts and crotches
and wait for them to circle like moons
or idle like spacecraft without enough fuel.

Where pendants won't pivot, they place their hands
and chant a mantra of nasal vowels
till the teacher intones, *Fly to your navels*
and flood them with beacons of radiant light.

Returning to earth, they pay the instructor,
purchase crystals on strings of beads,
and go home to loved ones who treat their afflictions
with marijuana and Johnny Walker.

THE MOURNER

Half the time flapping,
half the time limp,
she flies at half-mast
on a cardboard pole.

Her slumber boils
in bottomless pots
she can't remove
from memory's stove.

She craves the broth
of companionship
but chokes on even
a tiny sip.

And yet she studies,
jogs and shops,
dines with friends
and plays her flute

to please a world
terrified
of looking sorrow
in the eye.

TRIUMPH

When daybreak's plows
entombed the car
beside the curb,
we suited up
in nylon puff
and walked to school
through diamond dunes
that seemed to shout
Begin anew.

My son, exuberant,
plunged into fluff,
losing his feet,
his calves, his knees.
He shunned the path
I forged for him
as if it were strewn
with his sister's dolls

and made his way,
puffing, reddening,
falling and falling
till every inch
of his mummied physique
was white as his soul
at six years old.

Arriving at last
in shivers and sweat,
he greeted his teacher

with exaltation
that dwarfed the drifts
he'd overpowered
on his own.

POPCORN

Darling of sports fans
    of movie viewers
        of cramming students

it's born with teeth
    intact, yet yellowed
        like a crone's.

Swaddled in silk
    it sleeps in its crib
        until it dries behind the ears.

Poured in the popper
    it drums to signal
        its imminent stunt

then starts to jump
    like a tumbler
        on a trampoline

breathing harder
    with every leap
        till all at once

its muscles flag
    and its toughness turns
        to tow-headed fluff

fired into a buttery bowl,
    exuding the feel-good
        fragrance of crunch.

TERMINAL TWO

Business trip. Flight delayed.
The wand waved over my pin-striped suit
does not detect my aggravation.

Beside a pile of plastic bins, I dress
for the second time today,
trading sympathetic smiles
with other beltless, shoeless souls,
and stroll down a concourse teeming
with wheels. The air is dense
with the scent of impatience.

Cell phones flaunt vitality
at their aged fathers on the wall.
Vendors dispense an indulgence of donuts,
hot dogs, lattes, Cokes, and beers
to the sandaled and the cowboy-booted,
the yarmulked and baseball-capped.

Beyond a yellow *wet floor* sign,
I stand in a line as long as a runway,
watching women comb their hair
and fix their makeup in queasy light.
I drag my suitcase into a stall
designed for Lilliputian girls
and wave at a sensor as if I were saying
good-bye from the deck of the QE2.
The sheath on the seat does not advance.

Drowning out the tap of laptops,
a disembodied voice announces

mass in the chapel in fifteen minutes.
It calls Mrs. Jones to the courtesy phone,
warns against picking up orphaned bags.

Stranded on this Dali canvas,
I plunk myself down in a ketchup-stained seat
and lift my eyes to the nearest TV,
which reports that airfares are on the rise.

POSTPARTUM DEPRESSION

Once my wife was a carnival,
impish as a fun house mirror,
with wit that barked *C'mon and play*
and interests assorted as carousel horses.

But when our firstborn child came,
the carnival moved to another town,
leaving behind an empty field
smattered with melted ice cream bars,
trampled cotton candy cones,
tickets torn and soaked with rain.

Straining to hear calliope music,
I cradle our son and wonder if ever
he'll savor the taste of a taffy apple
or hold a spray of rainbow balloons.

DREAMS

When Night has basted
the house with hush

it raids the basket
of my brain, rummaging

through spools of black,
baby blue and molten red,

through hooks and snaps and safety pins,
needles with unseeing eyes,

through jagged scraps of taffeta,
burlap, gingham, velvet, fleece.

Then Night creates a crazy quilt
it tucks around me, wondering

if when I wake I'll choose to hang
its handiwork upon my wall

or stuff it in a plastic bag
intended for the Goodwill truck.

KEEPING UP

It doesn't matter what's under our feet—
the butcher's sawdust-sprinkled floor,
the gravel path to the jungle gym,
the sidewalk of a city street.
She walks a yard ahead of me,
her full skirt swishing against her matching
Bakelite bag.

Slow down, Mommy, I bleat

but she ignores my plea as if it were
a fly, a breeze, a falling leaf.
I lengthen my stride, wishing
that my sneakers were equipped with wheels.
A lace comes loose, but I don't dare
to stop and fix it, lest she
disappear forever from my life.

I eat my spinach, drink my milk,
hoping that my legs will grow
so I won't have to walk
                                    alone.

WHEN A PARENT PASSES

The one who wakes
in dream-drenched dark
to clean up vomit
and lay cool cloths
on burning skin

who makes the oatmeal
and tucks a note
in the brown bag lunch

who divides like a cell
into multiple selves
that commute to work
and wash the clothes
and cheer the team on
in the hot school gym

must brave the scowls
the rolling eyes
the insolence honed
on the wheel of grief

while the one who sleeps
in dreamless dark
is sainted

not

for healing the sick
feeding the hungry
or miracle-izing

but just for dying

REMINDER

I stroll through a neighborhood
greened by summer's
jealousy of spring's pastels.
Peonies droop their fuchsia heads,
as if ashamed of their radiance.
Evening drapes the clouds in shawls
of orange and pink. A blackbird
claims a ginkgo branch
whose leaves will fan tomorrow's heat.

Beside a curb, a squirrel sprawls,
its bloody body summoning flies.
I aim my eyes at a nearby yard
and scrutinize the roses there
while thorns form in my gut and throat.

My feet become concrete
as in a nightmare where I cannot flee.
I concentrate on a wrestling match
between a woman and a hose,
focus on a Frisbee game
between a boy and a chocolate Lab.

But something I don't understand
repeatedly propels my gaze
to the pulpy paws, the severed tail,
the pearl of an eye now lusterless.

CHANGE OF VENUE

Weary of her gilded frame,
she tiptoes out
of the family portrait
where generations
dressed in white
line up in rows
like bowling pins
against a background
of muted black,
every smile
slightly blurred.

She marches into
another photo
rimmed in oak
with glare-free glass,
where blemishes revel
in natural light
and every button
is in focus.

REPRIEVE FROM DEMENTIA

Mem'ries light the corners of my mind,
misty water-colored mem'ries of the way we were.

—Barbra Streisand

When her thoughts became a flurry of flakes
that melted as they hit the ground,
my white-haired mother forgot my face,
forgot the voice that clinched my fame.

We'd sit together drinking tea,
conversation impossible
as stopping trees from dropping leaves,
when suddenly she'd start to hum
a lullaby from her childhood,
pure white notes that buried our silence
in drifts of joy and peacefulness.

I'd harmonize and bless the Muse
of Music for the path she'd cleared
between two women stranded alone
on opposite sides of memory.

LATE BLOOMER

He phones from the party
at half past nine,
pleading for me
to pick him up
in a whisper
I can hardly hear.

I speed to a stucco
volcano of sound
where couples dance
in flashing light,
molten as lava,
cool as ash.

I summon him;
he fusses
so his friends will be sure
to hear his distress,
then shuffles
into darkness flecked
with fireflies

and bursts into tears,
sparking my memory
of what it is like
to be ripening slowly
inside a cocoon
while everyone else
is flying away.

GRIEF

It usually swims beneath the ripples,
tides, and swells of daily life,
its bloodless scales and pointy teeth
invisible as ocean salt.

But now and then it jumps like a whale
and splashes your eyes with stinging brine
before it takes a downward plunge.

You cast a line, desperate
to strip it clean of guts and bones,
to watch its eyes cloud over
as your heart has done so many times.

It shuns your bait, repeating its stunt
like an athlete training to win the Gold,
till inexplicably, it leaves.

You re-adjust your rudder and keel,
shift your jib to catch the breeze,
and forget the creature destined
to resurface when you least expect.

PACKING FOR SCHOOL

Open boxes flock on your floor
like monarchs about to migrate south.
An unfinished project due at the office,
piles of bills and unread statements
doze on my desk as I sit on your bed
and wrap my sadness in bubbly chatter.

Watching you pack your photos from prom,
your music collection, your high-heeled shoes,
I remember the time you sat in a cart
and repeatedly kicked off your tiny boots
while my patience grew talons and pointy teeth.

As my scolding crescendoed, a stranger crossed
the crowded supermarket aisle
and told me to treasure my time with you—
that you'd be grown
before I reached the check-out line.
I wanted to punch her in the nose,

but now I know that she was right.

APRIL'S CHILDREN

Crocus

Snow-haters' darling
defies groundhog prophecies
concerning winter

Forsythia

Cauldron of curry
spices up the bland landscape,
even if served cold

Daffodil

Yellow periscope
rises from its muddy sub
to spy on the sun

Tulip

Spring's snooty beauty
stands aloof as a blueblood,
her nose in the air

Hyacinth

Overdue mother
too distended with fragrance
to stay on her feet

ALTAR TALK

I

Being a man was easy
in the days when my hair
was dark as the dirt
in my fingernails. I never
missed a duck or deer, always
fixed the car myself, bested
the guys in bowling and pool.

Every time I cracked
the whip, my feelings
stayed within the ring,
wild tigers trained to obey,

until my oldest daughter laid
my newborn grandson
in my arms, and I cried
the tears of a woman, tears

that still attack
when I least expect—
during a movie, the nightly news,
a conversation with a friend.

I bow my head and beg You
to subdue the waves before my Self
erodes away.

II

When I created Adam, I
did not intend for Man to drown
emotion in the undertow.

The very tears that make you blush
are a gift from the boy whose birth released
the swell once trapped behind your dam,

a boy who will need a real man
to show him how to fling the cloak
of masculinity into the surf

and bask, stark naked, on the beach.

MOTHER

I am the pool's perimeter,
four right angles
linked by tile
grouted with devotion.

From my lap my children
dangle their ankles
in turquoise chill
till their shivers change
into eagerness,
and goggle-less,
they dive into diamonds,
unperturbed
by ropes and buoys.

Every so often
they paddle back,
grab for me
and take a breath,
then push away so hard
I chip,

unaware
that sometimes kicks
can lead to cracking
hard to patch.

YOUR HAND

with its nails obsessively clipped,
its pinkie burled with a writer's bump
you gnawed when you were nervous or bored,
its talent for widening eyes with a wand

is the only hand I want to grab
as I watch our daughter cross the stage,
beaming as she shakes the hand
of the hooded dean who bestows her diploma.

Other hands are free for the taking—
hands of relatives and friends
who've traveled here from far away
to cheer in the stadium of my pride.

But only yours, which Gaia holds,
can make this joyful moment whole,
and so it will be with each milestone
our children set in tomorrow's ring.

AIDS

The rapist rampages through Africa,
impregnating nations with babies
who will rock themselves
in one-room huts
where chaos is the only parent,
who will learn
to fire a rifle at ten,
to spread their prepubescent legs,
to think of death as a cliché

while across the waves
the grown bemoan
their acutely dysfunctional childhoods
over cappuccino and Chardonnay.

EMANCIPATION

The class clambers out
of the yellow bus
into the hush
of the Japanese Garden
in weather as flawless
as newly-raked sand.

I am six,
in a shirtwaist and socks
of identical hue,
the scuffs on my saddle shoes
covered with polish,
my ribboned braids
as tight as the girdle
my mother tugs over
her tummy each day.

The teacher claps.
We form a line
and walk down a path
to a rippleless pond
where lippy fish
orbit each other
like orange moons.
I wonder if they crave
the sea, the salty taste
of open space.

Directed to draw,
I study the evergreens,

pruned precisely
and wired to the earth
lest they try to escape
to a forest where trees
can caress the clouds,
can kiss the sun.

Seized by an urge
to abandon my crayons,
I run past a lantern,
a bamboo fence,
a trickling fountain,
a rounded bridge,
to a hill beyond
the garden's gate.

I climb to the top,
lie down on my side,
and roll to the base
of the grassy slope,
staining my dress,
untying my bows,
again and again,
again and again.

WHAT MOVIES NEVER SHOW

He rings her bell, his fly unzipped.
She opens the door, her smile wide

as the hole in her hose. A label
peeks out of her low-cut dress.

At the restaurant, they slurp their soup.
She burns her tongue; he drips on his tie.

Each says *what?* a dozen times.
He cannot figure out the tip.

With salad greens between their teeth,
they stroll outside, their fingers twined.

She keeps releasing to scratch an itch.
He blows his nose like a trumpeting swan.

Back at her place, they cuddle and kiss.
Her lopsided lipstick tattoos his face.

Wedged between the couch and her back,
his arm goes numb as a winter toe.

He shakes it out, unzips her gown,
fumbles with hooks on her push-up bra.

She struggles to unbuckle his belt,
which has left a print on her stomach flesh,

and tugs the trousers he's sitting on.
He slides his hand between her legs,

where a pad as thick as his eagerness
catches effusions of viscous red.

She leads him to her unmade bed,
grabs a package of latex rolled

as tightly as clothes in a camper's pack.
He comes before he starts to thrust,

crawls under a blanket of gravelly snores.
Next morning they wake in a sewer of breath,

his scalp a jumble of pick-up sticks,
her eye makeup smeared like finger-paint.

They fight for the bathroom, then rush off to work
with a curt goodbye.

TREASURES

She rummages in the night table drawer
with hands that shake like her uneaten Jell-O.
Her nails, once buffed and painted red,
are tiny gravestones, rough and gray.

She hands me an envelope
crammed with the youth
of a man she will shortly join beneath
bouquets replaced each Saturday—
my spouse, her son.

I finger a newborn's beaded bracelet,
a ribboned chronicle of firsts:
the smile,
the tooth,
the solid food,
grammar school photos identically posed,
poetry penned in teenage script—
each more valuable to her
than the diamond in her wedding ring.

I promise to preserve them
and bequeath them to my children
for passing on
to sons and daughters of their own,

who probably will throw away
the relics of a relative
they never knew.

WHY I RARELY TRAVEL

I've slept in beds
the size of Europe,
with sheets as smooth
as a Japanese bow
and pillows soft
as Caribbean sand.

But my bed at home
is the only bed
where sleep lets down
its coiled hair
and tarantellas
to midnight's band.

I pull back the spread
that long ago
surrendered its stripes
to the washing machine.
A hot water bottle
beckons my feet
like an eager lover.
My Siamese
curls up at my neck,
a muffler crocheted
from skeins of purrs.

As an ancient pillow
cradles my head,
my eyelids shut
like cinema doors

and movies start
where I'm the star,

undisturbed
by home's familiar
creaks and groans,
concluding with a shock of light
and the tickle of whiskers
on my cheek.

I knew when you arrived that you would go,
that childhood is just a puff of smoke,
that fate will not maintain the status quo.

But living day-to-day is a plateau,
and busyness hides dread beneath a cloak.
I knew when you arrived that you would go,

that your departure would be apropos.
Yet part of me still hoped it was a joke
that fate will not maintain the status quo,

for as your mother, I had come to know
the tenderness and laughter you evoke.
I knew when you arrived that you would go

but told myself time's pocket watch was slow.
Then suddenly a voice began to croak
that fate will not maintain the status quo.

Loud and shrill the voice began to grow
until the crystal of my being broke.
I knew when you arrived that you would go,
that fate will not maintain the status quo.

FOR ANNE

Wherever a car bomb is exploding,
wherever bodies red and wet as the Devil's tears
are being dragged from a public bus,

wherever people are hurling curses
as if their words could propel the flying
rocks and bottles faster, farther,

there you are, mic in hand,
describing the scene
in a voice as cool as saxophone jazz.

You've shaken Death's hand
in Baghdad and Chechnya,
Afghanistan, Pakistan, Tiananmen Square

as if both of you
were ambassadors
asked to attend the same dinners of state.

I conjecture about a younger Anne,
who never said no to a playground dare
and rode the fastest roller coasters.

Maybe you drove a motorcycle
without a helmet or walked alone
at night in dubious neighborhoods.

Then again, it's possible

your youth was dull as a plotless drama,
drawing you to passion plays

or maybe you were teased for being
timid as an August drizzle
and want to prove your bravery.

Perhaps you yearn to putter
in a cozy home with reliable heat,
electric power and drinkable water

like me as I listen to your reports
each day while sipping safety
from a demitasse of jealousy.

OPEN STUDIO

Having finally mastered
the rigors of stick men and paint-by-number,
the wannabe artist— a color wheel
of eagerness and intimidation—
clips her paper to the board.

Around her, objects cluster like cliques:
saxophones, shells, and women's shoes,
vintage gloves and carved giraffes,
pyramids of cardboard boxes,
vases, apples, lemons, leaves.

The wannabe chooses a Number Six
from an overwhelm of eraserless pencils
and scrutinizes the bowler they told her
to draw without laying her gaze on the page.
She ventures a line that stumbles and veers
like a reveler chugging a six-pack of beer.
Next she is asked to draw a jacket
drooping from a wooden peg.
She squints at the garment as if she were trying
to read the last line on an eye doctor's chart.
Shadows she knows she's supposed to see
play hide and seek in the fabric's folds.

The wannabe furtively searches the room
for a picture-in-progress inferior to hers.
Eyeing creations of paint and pastel,
she feels like a guest attired in rags
at a gala where everyone's wearing a gown.

An hour later, her sketches are whisked
to the front of the room for the class to critique.
They cower behind a flamboyant collage
and pray for invisibility.

At the session's end, the wannabe slinks
to a garbage can in the parking lot.
She deposits her artwork and hurries home
to expertly draw

a bubble bath.

ST. VALENTINE'S DAY MASSACRE

Fourteenth day
of the second month.
A fat child opens
a shoebox pasted
with hearts and foil
clumsily cut
with blunt-edged scissors.
Only the teacher
has slipped an envelope
through the slot.

A husband flurries
like scuttlebutt
from shop to shop
at six o'clock,
willing to pay
whatever it takes
for roses to fill
the vase his wife
took out of the closet
the previous evening.
Every store
is bare as a garden
in February.

A graduate student
dabs perfume
behind her ears
and lights a scatter
of scented candles.

Her boyfriend calls;
he has to write
till dawn to finish
his thesis draft.
She corks the wine,
freezes the shrimp,
spends the evening
watching TV.

And a widow hermits
in her home
till the fifteenth day
of the second month,
fleeing scarlet
store displays
that seem to bellow
He is gone.

PREDICTABILITIES

Cottonwood trees paste Santa beards
on window screens

The next door neighbors deck their deck
with red geraniums

Bees convene like Legionnaires
in the grill's cold coals

Diva mowers throw their voices
into the hush of early evening

Predictabilities

Sanity savers

when cell phones poke their bony fingers
into our most private parts

when the six o'clock news delivers shocks
like a winter house

when recession's henchmen axe the factory
that fed the family for generations

when our pockets sag with the heaviness
of excess change

MAKING THE BEST OF WHAT IS LEFT

The woman's skin is a crumple of paper,
her eyes, a frustration of fuzziness.
Aches and pains have taken over
her days like a boss who baffles the office
by gradually changing established procedures.

The man's huge hands, once deft with a hammer,
have started to shake as he passes the butter.
His memory slips and slides and falls
like a child in a rink without his skates.

Yet when the man comes home each day,
spent from the job he refuses to leave,
the woman puts on Sinatra or Como,
cocks her head as she did in her youth,

and they fox trot through their bungalow
in the dimming light of late afternoon.

CRAZY

Yesterday I wriggled out
of winter's straightjacket,
laughing like a lunatic, and kissed

the first robin, the first green sprout.
Sunbeams patted my hatless head
as if to say, *Go play, you fool.*

Today I opened my bedroom blinds
to the sight of trees and grass as white
as asylum sheets.

Flakes the size of crocuses
jumped from the sky as if intent
on suicide.

So much like life, these Midwest Marches,
which loosen our restraints and then
re-bind us when we least expect.

FIRST FLU

Across the amber waves of grain
my daughter twists and turns in bed,
a highway paved with aches and pains.

Music blasts throughout her dorm,
hatcheting her spinning head.
Friends bring steaming mugs of news,
then vanish into books or beer
before she can pry a word of thanks
from a voice box nailed shut for days.

A bullhorn lodged within my chest
insists I take the next plane out
to bring Saltines and Gatorade,
to wipe her brow, to change her sheets.

But rescue's an addictive drug,
so from my kitchen in the East,
I comfort her by telephone.

CHANGING SIDES

Six months after she tucks her husband
into a bed of dirt and clay, resignation

wakes the rings asleep in one another's arms
for thirty years upon her hand. They squint

in the astringent light of early mourning,
longing for just a few more winks.

She slips the plain one over her knuckle, lays it
in a velvet box she buries in a dresser drawer.

The diamond ring balks at banishment
to a hand it wasn't meant to fit. It spins

on the pinkie, chafes the other fingers' skin.
But she forces it on and covers her ears

as her left side shrieks with the shock and rage
of the just-been-robbed.

SECOND TIME AROUND

The married-once
examine each other
for scratches and dents,

check for excessive mileage,
and take their turns at the steering wheel,
testing for responsiveness.

He promises to be in touch,
but her phone is mute as if her hope
had run over the ringer.

She dissects his silence like terms of a loan.
Is he mired in work? Sick with a cold?
Or did she kick his tires too hard?

Immobilized by the brake of the past,
she waits for him to make the next move,
worried he's seeking a better deal,

while he watches TV in his living room
and counts the days until he can call
without seeming too eager.

COLLEGE TOWN

In this city of brick where monuments
are commonplace as blades of grass
and everything proclaims to be
The Very First

I rarely see a wrinkled face,
a balding head, a stooped physique—
only flesh as bare and firm
as just-picked fruit,
pierced and patterned with tattoos
that would have made the Founders swoon.

No one here wears sensible shoes,
carries umbrellas, walks with canes.
Hair is never gray or white
but dyed or sprayed in rainbow hues.

How strange to feel so very old
as I stroll through streets
Revere once rode
and gaze at a bay where black tea steeped
centuries before my birth.

OFFERING

Poetry makes nothing happen.
               –W.H. Auden

This one's for you, the people
who don't read poetry,
who don't have time to read at all,
who may not even know how to read.

I see you when I buy a TV.
You are uncrating metal desks,
using your back instead of your knees.
You will never visit a chiropractor.

I see you when I stare out the window
in search of an elusive rhyme.
You are cutting my neighbor's grass,
conversing in a language I,
a master of language, cannot understand.

I see you from the podium
as I read my latest creation aloud.
You are mopping the bookstore floor.

I wish my stanzas could buy your children
winter coats, could free you from needing
to work on the Sabbath. But in your world,
poetry makes nothing happen,

so although I've said this one's for you,
both of us know it's really for me.